Ms. Frizzle's Adventures
ANCIENT EGYPT

Ms. Frizzle's Adventures
ANCIENT EGYPT

by JOANNA COLE
illustrated by BRUCE DEGEN

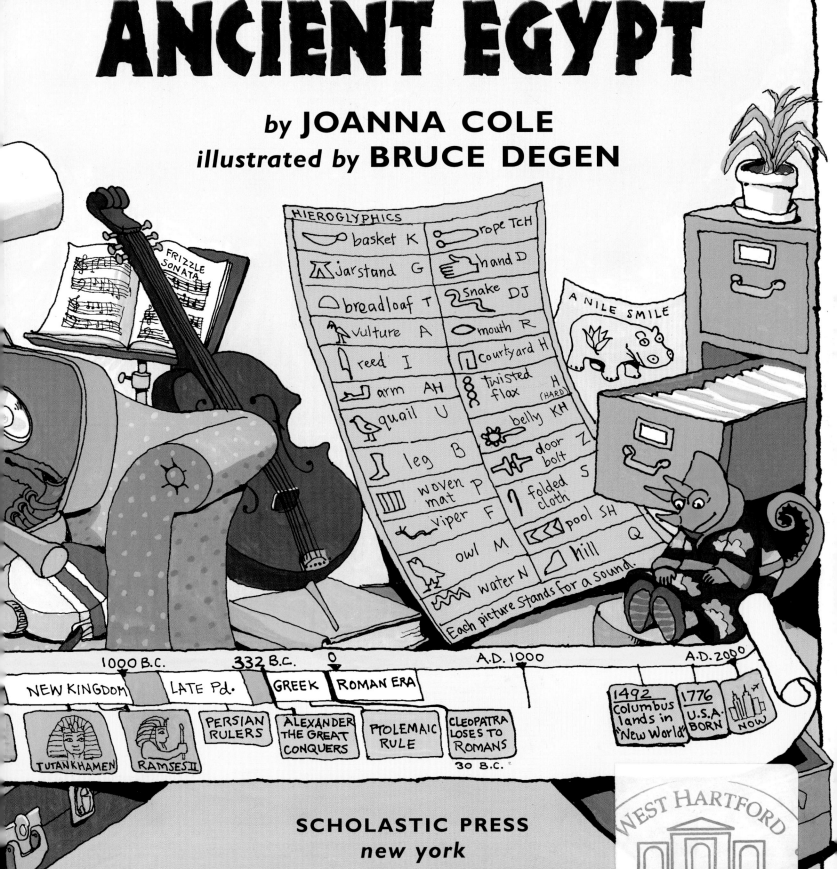

SCHOLASTIC PRESS
new york

The author thanks Magy and Mona, her tour guides in Egypt.
The author and illustrator would like to thank Dr. Phyllis Saretta an Egyptologist who
lectures at the Metropolitan Museum of Art, for her careful review of the manuscript and illustrations.

B

JQ
932
Cole

To my husband,
Phil, my favorite pharaoh.
—J.C.

To my wife, Chris,
we visited the pyramids on our first date;
they were just being built.
—B.D.

It was a long flight.
When night came, everyone fell asleep.
Well, *almost* everyone.

As the sun rose, we found ourselves flying over Egypt.
Down below, we saw the Nile River.
Green farms ran along either side of the river.
Beyond the farms, there was nothing but desert.
It was sand, sand, sand, as far as the eye could see.

Our group couldn't wait for the plane to land.
Fortunately, they didn't have to.
Somehow the airplane door swung open.
I can't imagine how that happened. Can you?
Thank goodness I had a supply of parachutes in my bag!

Herb, our tour guide, floated down into Cairo,
the capital city of modern Egypt.
But the rest of us were blown away by a gust of wind.

IN CAIRO THERE ARE AIRPORTS, TALL BUILDINGS, COMPUTERS, CARS, AND TRUCKS...

WHERE ARE YOU GOING

...PEOPLE ALSO USE CAMELS, DONKEYS, AND HORSES.

MODERN EGYPT IS A MIX OF OLD AND NEW!

MODERN EGYPT IS A LONG WAY DOWN!

EGYPT IN MODERN TIMES

Almost all Egyptians practice the Moslem religion...Islam.

The language of Egypt is Arabic.

في فصل الأستاذة «فار
شمق عن الحيوانات
شهر كامل وقد اتعبنا ذلك

All children learn English in school.

AaBb Cc Dd Ee Ff

THE MAGIC SCHOOL BUS

Here was where my years as a teacher really helped.
I knew a lot about Egypt,
so I took over where Herb left off.
With me on the job, something interesting was
bound to happen.

Sure enough, something interesting did happen.
As our feet reached the ground,
the cars and trucks disappeared.
So did the modern people.
Even the horses and camels were gone.
We were back in ancient Egypt.
I can't imagine how that happened. Can you?

IN THE AGE OF PYRAMIDS, THERE WERE NO CAMELS OR HORSES IN EGYPT. THEY CAME LATER.

THERE WERE NO TOURISTS FROM THE 21ST CENTURY, EITHER.

WE CAME LATER, TOO.

EGYPT IN ANCIENT TIMES

ANCIENT EGYPTIANS USED A LANGUAGE THAT IS NO LONGER SPOKEN.

THEY HAD THEIR OWN RELIGION AND WORSHIPPED MANY GODS.

KING OF GODS
RE

Re, the sun god, was the creator of the universe and father of all the gods.

ANCIENT EGYPTIANS HAD STYLES OF DRESS ALL THEIR OWN.

THEY WORE BEAUTIFUL JEWELRY.

THEIR EYE MAKEUP WAS CALLED KOHL. IT WAS A COSMETIC AND AN ANTISEPTIC. IT MAY HAVE PROTECTED AGAINST EYE INFECTIONS.

We would have looked pretty funny in our modern clothes. Fortunately, I had a supply of costumes in my bag, so we looked just like the ancient Egyptians.

WHO ARE THOSE STRANGE PEOPLE?

I DON'T KNOW.

THEY SURE DON'T LOOK LIKE ANCIENT EGYPTIANS!

STYLE FROM THE NILE

CHILD'S SIDE HAIR KNOT

SOME PEOPLE SHAVED THEIR HEADS. OTHERS WORE WIGS.

ANCIENT EGYPTIANS ALSO HAD THEIR OWN STYLE OF ART. WHEN THEY DREW PICTURES OF PEOPLE, THEY COMBINED FRONT AND SIDE VIEWS. THEY THOUGHT THIS GAVE THE BEST VIEW OF EACH PART.

Head is shown from the side.

Eyes drawn as if seen from the front

Shoulders and chest from front.

Hips, legs, and feet from side.

An ancient Egyptian town was a busy place
Children were playing. Craftspeople were working.
We saw a bakery and a brewery in operation.
Everywhere people were buying and selling things.

My Travel Diary by Rasheeda
In the marketplace we saw
• Bakers making bread from wheat and barley.
• Brewers making beer from fermented bread.
• Scribes writing down how many loaves of bread and how many jars of beer were made.
• Farmers selling animals, fruit, and vegetables.
• Craftspeople making pottery, linen cloth, sandals, baskets, and jewelry.
• Children playing many games.

BREAD BAKED IN BELL-SHAPED JARS

BEER MAKERS

SCRIBES

MIXING YEAST

FARMERS

Ancient Egyptians did not have money, so people traded what they had for what they needed. Workers of all kinds often got paid in bread and beer. They used some of their wages to feed their families. They spent the rest on other things.

Ancient Egyptians wrote on paper made from papyrus, a large water plant. The paper was called papyrus, too.

I'M GROWING PAPYRUS IN MY POOL.

I'M WRITING ABOUT HIS POOL ON PAPYRUS.

MAKING PAPYRUS

① STALKS CUT INTO SHORT SECTIONS.

② GREEN OUTSIDE IS REMOVED. INNER FIBERS SLICED AND POUNDED FLAT.

③ SECOND LAYER LAID CROSSWISE...

AND POUNDED ON.

④ SURFACE POLISHED SMOOTH WITH A STONE.

SHEETS GLUED TOGETHER TO MAKE A SCROLL.

BRUSH CASE

BRUSHES MADE FROM SOFTENED REEDS

WATER JAR

PALETTE

BLACK INK
RED INK

HIEROGLYPH FOR "SCRIBE"

Most ancient Egyptians could not read or write, so they hired writers called scribes to help. Scribes wrote letters, kept records, figured out how much tax people owed, and lettered religious texts. We visited a school for scribes. With all my teaching experience, I was a big help!

CLICK!

NO TALKING, PLEASE!

LET ME HELP. TRY IT THIS WAY, BEKU.

WHO IS THIS STRANGE PERSON?

STUDENTS WROTE ON WOODEN BOARDS WHICH WERE CLEANED AND REUSED

MEANWHILE, IN MODERN EGYPT, HERB VISITS THE CAIRO MUSEUM...

ANCIENT EGYPT WAS THE FIRST PLACE IN THE WORLD WHERE WRITING WAS USED WIDELY. SCRIBES WERE EVERYWHERE!

HELP! I LOST MY TOUR GROUP!

CAIRO MUSEUM

3 KINDS OF ANCIENT EGYPTIAN WRITING:

① HIEROGLYPHICS: Each symbol stood for a sound, just like our letters. Used for religious writings.

a b K d i g h y

STATUE OF SCRIBE

② HIERATIC: Used for government business.

a b k d i f

③ DEMOTIC: Used in everyday life.

a b K d i f

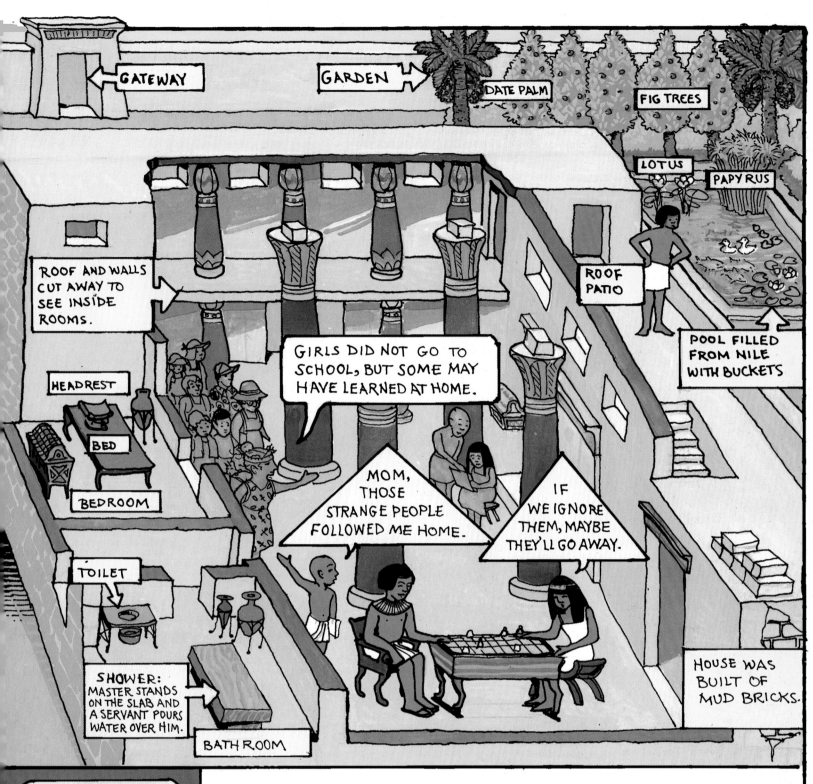

GATEWAY

GARDEN

DATE PALM

FIG TREES

LOTUS

PAPYRUS

ROOF AND WALLS CUT AWAY TO SEE INSIDE ROOMS.

ROOF PATIO

POOL FILLED FROM NILE WITH BUCKETS

HEADREST

GIRLS DID NOT GO TO SCHOOL, BUT SOME MAY HAVE LEARNED AT HOME.

BED

BEDROOM

MOM, THOSE STRANGE PEOPLE FOLLOWED ME HOME.

IF WE IGNORE THEM, MAYBE THEY'LL GO AWAY.

TOILET

SHOWER: MASTER STANDS ON THE SLAB AND A SERVANT POURS WATER OVER HIM.

HOUSE WAS BUILT OF MUD BRICKS.

BATH ROOM

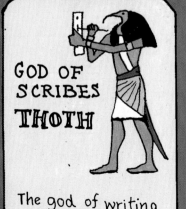

GOD OF SCRIBES
THOTH

The god of writing was often shown as a man with an ibis head.

After school, we went home with a boy named Beku.
His father, Ramose, was a wealthy scribe
who could afford a large house.
It even had a stone bathroom where servants
poured water over their master.
This was perhaps the world's first shower!
Ramose enjoyed playing *senet* — a popular board game —
with his wife, Meryt.

Beku's family seemed busy, so we decided to leave. On the road there was a farm family going home from the market.
Our group didn't want to miss anything, so we joined them.

The crops were ready to harvest.
I encouraged everyone in our group to pitch in.
We had just brought in the last of the wheat,
when the Nile started overflowing its banks.

The farmers weren't surprised when the Nile flooded.
In ancient Egypt, this happened every year.
Later, when the water drew back, it left rich mud
that fertilized the fields.
The flood made the farmers happy because it meant
good crops the next year.
It made me happy because I got to teach about it!
And it made our group happy because they love learning!

The barge was carrying stones to build a pyramid
— a tomb where an Egyptian king would be buried.
The pyramid was built in the desert.
No floodwater came there so work could go on
all year without stopping.
The ancient Egyptians had not invented wheels,
so they had to drag the stones along on the ground.

People often think the pyramids were made by slaves, but that isn't true.
Pyramid builders were paid in bread and beer, just like other workers.

Nile

Canal

Harbor

Canal and harbor were built to bring boats and stone barges closer to pyramid sites.

The pharaoh

Architect: designer of pyramid

My Travel Diary
by Rasheeda
The white crown was the crown of southern Egypt.
The red crown was the crown of northern Egypt.
The pharaoh was king of all Egypt, so he wore both—the double crown.

Vizier: chief of all the kings work.

ANCIENT EGYPTIANS BELIEVED THEIR KING HAD DIVINE POWERS.

Imagine how excited we were when we saw the pharaoh's boat landing at the dock.
The pharaoh was king of all Egypt.
It was his pyramid, and he wanted to see the work in progress.

GOD OF THE SKY HORUS

Ancient Egyptians thought their pharaoh was an earthly form of the sky god.

CAT GODDESS BASTET

Late in ancient Egypt's history, people worshipped a cat goddess. Because of her, they thought some cats were holy.

CLICK!

SHALL WE DANCE?

ANCIENT EGYPTIANS SURE KNEW HOW TO HAVE FUN!

ME, TOO!

ME, THREE!

PARTY ANIMALS

Unfortunately, the pharaoh became ill at the end of the party. His wife and son helped him to bed.

The next morning there was a big commotion in the palace.
The old pharaoh had died in the night.
Everyone was weeping and wailing.

Ancient Egyptians believed in life after death.
But they thought this was possible only if
a person's dead body did not decay.
That's why priests preserved the pharaoh's body
by making it into a mummy.
I knew that, at this sad time, they would be
grateful for all the help they could get.

6. Put magic charms called amulets among the wrappings to protect the mummy.

Scarab = rebirth

Eye of Horus = protection

Ankh = The breath of life

5. Remove body from salt and wrap in strips of linen cloth.

AREN'T WE LUCKY TO SHARE IN THE EXPERIENCE OF MUMMIFICATION?

CLICK!

7. Cover the face with a beautiful mummy mask.

8. Place the mummy in a beautiful mummy case.

MEANWHILE IN MODERN EGYPT, HERB VIEWS EXHIBIT OF OBJECTS FOUND IN TOMBS.

Clothes

Cosmetics

Musical Instruments

Writing materials

Games

Furniture

ALONG WITH THE MUMMY, ANCIENT EGYPTIANS BURIED THINGS THE DEAD PERSON WOULD NEED IN THE AFTERLIFE.

ANIMAL FIGURES

A funeral boat carried the mummy to the pyramid, which was gleaming in the sun. Weeping relatives and funeral dancers followed the coffin.

TEMPLE IN FRONT OF PYRAMID

My Travel Diary by Rasheeda
The mummy was put on the funeral boat.

There was a large funeral procession.

The coffin was pulled by oxen.

In the temple, priests performed religious ceremonies.
After the funeral, the mummy was sealed up in the pyramid.
Now the king's son would become the new pharaoh.
The old pharaoh, the Egyptians believed,
would live forever in the afterworld.

"YOU WILL LIVE AGAIN. YOU WILL LIVE FOREVER. YOU WILL BE YOUNG AGAIN FOREVER."

• The funeral ceremony was performed in the temple.

• We saw the ceremony called "The opening of the Mouth." A priest touched the mummy's mouth with a special wand. Egyptians believed the pharaoh could then eat and drink and speak in the afterlife.

• The burial chamber was inside the pyramid.

GOD OF THE AFTERWORLD
OSIRIS

Mummy-shaped Osiris ruled the land of the dead. His skin was green, the color of plants, which may have represented new life for the dead.

COULD IT REALLY HAPPEN?

If you went on a trip to Egypt, you might have many exciting adventures. But there are some things that can't happen anywhere.

FOR INSTANCE:

▲ You can't really go back in time.

▲ The door of an airplane won't open so easily, even if there is turbulence.

▲ A lizard – no matter how cute she is – does not wear clothes or act like a human in any other ways.

▲ Many events in this book could not be completed during a short school vacation. In real life, they would take months or even years.

> **for example:**
> ◆ It took ancient Egyptian embalmers seven and a half weeks to mummify a dead body.
> ◆ It took six months for the Nile to reach full flood stage.
> ◆ It took twenty years or more to build a pyramid.

▲ The pyramids were built at the beginning of ancient Egyptian history, but some of the scenes in this book are from later times, when styles were more elaborate. The pictures of the pharaoh's boat, the banquet, and the funeral all show styles that were popular thousands of years after the age of pyramids. Even though this is not really accurate in terms of time, we wanted to show readers the richness of ancient Egyptian civilization.

▲ And, last but not least, all those parachutes and stuff would never fit into one small backpack!